T0389990

THE
APACHE

BY BETTY MARCKS

CONSULTANT: TIM TOPPER,
CHEYENNE RIVER SIOUX

BLASTOFF!
DISCOVERY

BELLWETHER MEDIA • MINNEAPOLIS, MN

Blastoff! Discovery launches a new mission: reading to learn. Filled with facts and features, each book offers you an exciting new world to explore!

BLASTOFF! UNIVERSE

GRADE K

GRADES 1-3

GRADE 4

Author's Statement of Positionality:
I am a white woman of European descent. As such, I can claim no direct lived experience of being a Native American. In writing this book, however, I have tried to be an ally by relying on sources by Native American writers and authors whenever possible and have worked to let their voices guide its content.

This edition first published in 2026 by Bellwether Media, Inc.

Library of Congress Cataloging-in-Publication Data

LC record for The Apache available at: https://lccn.loc.gov/2025018381

Editor: Elizabeth Neuenfeldt   Series Designer: Andrea Schneider
Book Designer: Laura Sowers

Printed in the United States of America, North Mankato, MN.

TABLE OF CONTENTS

THE PEOPLE

The Apache are a group of Native American nations. The nations have similar but varied **cultures** and **traditions**. Apache peoples are **descendants** of speakers of Athabaskan languages. These speakers were from the subarctic areas of today's Canada and Alaska. People often refer to members of the nations as Apache. But members may prefer to be called a form of the word *Nde*. It means "The People."

The homelands of many Apache nations span the southern **Great Plains**. They also include parts of today's Southwestern United States. Some Apache homelands stretch into Mexico.

COLORADO

N
W + E
S

ARIZONA

OKLAHOMA

NEW
MEXICO

TEXAS

■ HOMELAND OF ATHABASKAN LANGUAGE SPEAKERS BEFORE 1500 CE

APACHE NAME

The name *Apache* may come from a Zuni word meaning "enemy." The Zuni are Native American peoples from the Southwestern U.S.

GREAT PLAINS

TRADITIONAL APACHE LIFE

MESCALERO APACHE

Athabaskan peoples began moving south from northwestern North America before 1400 CE. They likely moved because of conflicts from warring tribes. They settled in areas of today's Southwestern U.S. and Great Plains. They formed their own cultural groups. The groups became the Navajo Nation, Lipan Apache, Chiricahua Apache, Mescalero Apache, Jicarilla Apache, and Plains Apache. Other Apache groups formed as well.

Many Apache groups were further divided into **bands**. They shared cultural practices. Bands often included women's extended families. Men joined their wives' families after marriage.

LANGUAGE FAMILY

The Athabaskan language family is one of the largest in North America. It includes around 38 languages.

TIPIS

The daily life of **ancestral** Apache peoples varied. It was based on where they lived and the traditions of their bands. Many Apache bands moved often. Plains Apache often lived in tipis. These houses were made of animal hides. They could be moved from place to place. Some ancestral Apache built *wickiups*. These houses were dome-shaped and made of branches. They were also easy to move.

Ancestral Apache hunted and gathered foods and goods. Some nations learned to farm. They grew corn, beans, squash, and other crops.

FORBIDDEN ANIMALS

Contacting or being near certain animals was back luck for some ancestral Apache. They stayed away from snakes, owls, coyotes, and bears.

APACHE RESOURCES

OAK OR WILLOW POLES

STRANDS OF YUCCA

BRUSH OR ANIMAL HIDES

WICKIUP

Chiricahua Apache people were skilled **raiders**. Bands that traveled could not carry large amounts of food and other goods. They relied on raiding when supplies were low. They often gathered cattle, horses, and food. Raiders could quietly take what they needed and escape unseen. Raids were rarely violent.

Ancestral Apache were often known for being skilled warriors as well. Warriors were trained to know the land. They could blend in with their surroundings. They kept their people and their land safe.

ILLUSTRATION OF GERONIMO RETURNING FROM A RAID

CHIRICAHUA MOUNTAINS

EUROPEAN CONTACT

Apache and European relationships largely started in the late 1500s. Some bands had mostly peaceful trades with the Spanish. But conflict grew as the Spanish and Apache raided each other.

ORIGINAL APACHE TERRITORY TAKEN OVER BY SETTLERS IN THE 1800S

Apache life changed more in the 1800s. The Mexican government made **bounties** in the 1830s and 1840s to stop raids. Bounty hunters looked to capture any Apache people they could find. Meanwhile, the U.S. government continued its push westward. Some Apache bands worked with the U.S. during the **Mexican-American War**. Then, **settlers** flooded Apache **territory** after the discovery of gold in California in 1848.

Apache peoples wanted to keep their lands and people safe. In the mid-1800s, conflicts broke out between the U.S. and Apache groups. This became known as the **Apache Wars**. Chiricahua Chief Cochise was one Apache leader during this time. He led many raids against the U.S. in the 1860s. Geronimo was another Chiricahua Apache leader around this time. He led his followers against the U.S. military for many years.

FAMOUS APACHE

GERONIMO

BIRTHDAY   June 1829

DEATH   February 17, 1909

FAMOUS FOR

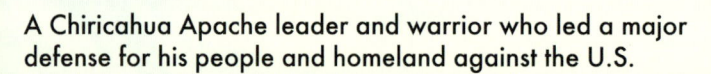

A Chiricahua Apache leader and warrior who led a major defense for his people and homeland against the U.S.

GERONIMO AND OTHER
APACHE WARRIORS

But the U.S. began forcing Apache peoples onto
reservations. Apache peoples were forced to
depend on the U.S. to survive. But they did not lose
hope. They worked to keep their cultures alive.

Today, at least 129,000 people identify as Apache. Many are members of one of nine federally recognized Apache nations. These nations all have reservations. A few share reservations with other nations. Reservations are in the states of Arizona, New Mexico, and Oklahoma. There are also Apache nations that are recognized by their respective states.

Some members of Apache nations live on reservations. Other members live and work throughout the U.S. and other countries.

APACHE RESERVATIONS IN NEW MEXICO

NEW MEXICO

■ JICARILLA APACHE NATION
■ MESCALERO APACHE TRIBE

Apache nations have their own governments. They work for the people. Many of the nations have Tribal **Councils**. These councils are led by a president or chairperson. The nations have committees that provide services to help their members live well. These may include education and health services. Some nations have committees to keep their lands safe. Nations may also have cultural committees that keep their traditions alive.

GOVERNMENT OF THE YAVAPAI-APACHE NATION

TRIBAL COUNCIL
- Chairperson
- Vice Chairperson
- 9-member council

JUDICIAL BRANCH
- Tribal Court
- Court of Appeals

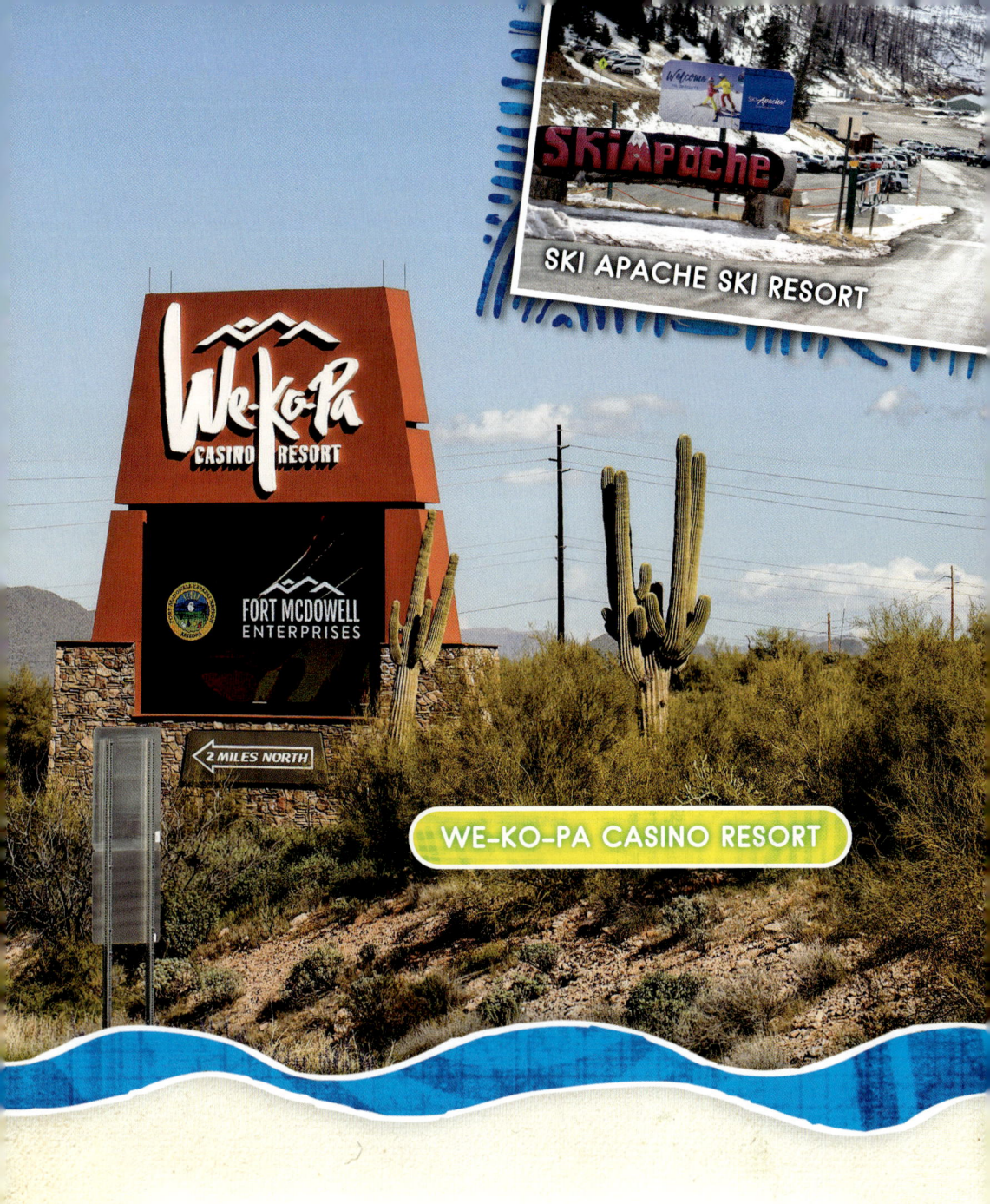

SKI APACHE SKI RESORT

WE-KO-PA CASINO RESORT

2 MILES NORTH

Many nations have strong economies. Tribal businesses such as casinos, resorts, and other attractions help Apache nations grow.

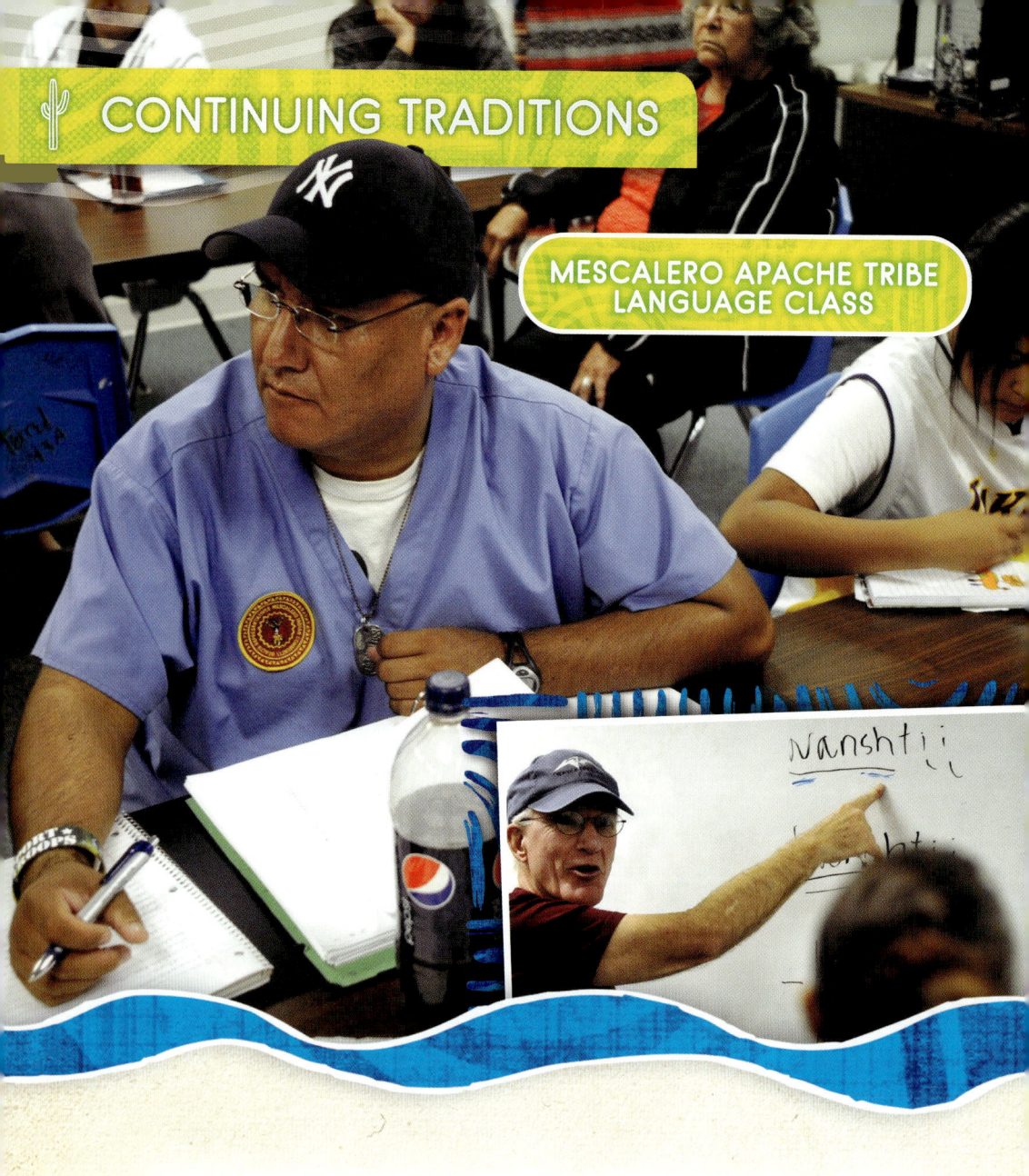

MESCALERO APACHE TRIBE LANGUAGE CLASS

Apache nations make sure their members can practice their cultures and traditions. Some nations have cultural programs. The programs offer classes to members. The Fort Sill Apache Tribe hosts classes in how to make different traditional items. These include jewelry, clothing, and Chiricahua beadwork.

Many nations have language programs. People can learn the language of their ancestors. Some programs keep Apache languages alive in other ways. The Mescalero Apache Tribe records the Apache language and history of their people. They also make lessons for schools to include in classrooms.

APACHE BEADWORK

Apache peoples have decorated clothes, jewelry, and other items with detailed beadwork for centuries.

MESCALERO APACHE NECKLACE

JICARILLA APACHE MOCCASINS

CHIRICAHUA APACHE WAR CAP

Many Apache nations run their own museums. This helps to protect their cultures and traditions. The White Mountain Apache Cultural Center keeps important items safe. It also helps people in the community and beyond learn about the nation's history and traditions.

Ceremonies are another way people honor their heritage. The Mescalero Apache honor girls becoming adults with a four-day ceremony. People share songs, dances, and prayers to bring the girl a long life. The ceremony is also said to bring good things to the community.

POW WOWS

Some Apache nations host Pow Wows. These gatherings often include traditional dancing, clothing, and food. Pow Wows are one way people of many different nations come together to celebrate their cultures.

FIGHT TODAY, BRIGHT TOMORROW

DROUGHT ON
JICARILLA APACHE LAND

Apache nations are experiencing the negative effects of **climate change**. Warmer and drier weather patterns are creating longer summers and shorter winters. They are causing more **droughts** and wildfires. These changes are affecting tribal economies, water supplies, crops, and more.

But Apache nations are taking action. The Mescalero Apache Tribe's Department of Resource Management and the U.S. Forest Service manage wildfires together. They use Tribal knowledge and western science to make ecosystems healthy. They use controlled burns and other practices that help prevent major wildfires.

MEMBER OF THE MESCALERO APACHE TRIBE WORKING WITH THE U.S. FOREST SERVICE

WILDFIRE

The U.S. government's mistreatment toward Native American peoples has created lasting damage. Many people living on reservations experience **poverty**. The limits on resources, jobs, and cultural practices are felt by many.

HEALTHY, LOCAL FOODS

Mike Montoya is leader of the Mescalero Tribal Fish Hatchery and Sovereign Nations Service Corps. He also leads a farm-to-table program. It produces healthy, local foods. It also created composting and recycling programs.

WHITE MOUNTAIN APACHE RESERVATION

Many Apache nations are fighting back. Programs such as the Yavapai Indian Foundation work to strengthen community members. They keep traditions. They also provide job training. The White Mountain Apache Tribe works with the First Things First program. They make sure children are given opportunities to live well. Their work gives hope for a bright future!

BY THE 1730s

The Spanish begin building forts and placing troops to limit Apache raids

BEFORE 1400

Ancestral Apache peoples move to areas of today's southern and southwestern regions of the U.S. and northern Mexico

1871

General George Crook takes around 50 men from Fort Apache to serve as Apache Scouts during the Apache Wars

BY THE 1700s

Some Apache groups take part in raids in what is now Mexico

1862

Chief Conchise and Chief Mangas lead the largest war party of the Apache Wars in the Battle of the Apache Pass

1872 TO 1875

U.S. army troops force Mescalero Apache and Lipan Apache peoples onto a reservation in New Mexico

2024

The group Apache Stronghold asks the U.S. Supreme Court to hear their case against a copper mine that could destroy a holy Apache site in New Mexico

1924

Apache people become U.S. citizens due to the Indian Citizenship Act, but most continue to endure harsh living conditions at the hands of the U.S. government

1886

Geronimo surrenders during the last major battle of the Apache Wars

1981

The Fort McDowell Yavapai Nation successfully stops the Orme Dam project, protecting their homelands from destruction

GLOSSARY

ancestral—related to relatives who lived long ago

Apache Wars—a series of conflicts between Apache tribes and the U.S. military between 1849 and 1886 with smaller conflicts occurring until 1924

bands—groups of people who live as communities and share cultures

bounties—payments for capturing people

ceremonies—sets of actions performed in a particular way, often as part of religious or spiritual worship

climate change—a human-caused change in Earth's weather due to warming temperatures

councils—groups of people who meet to run governments

cultures—the beliefs, arts, and ways of life in places or societies

descendants—people related to a person or group of people who lived at an earlier time

droughts—extended periods of time with little to no rainfall

Great Plains—a region of flat or gently rolling land in the central United States and parts of southern Canada

Mexican-American War—a conflict between the United States and Mexico that took place from 1846 to 1848

poverty—the lack of money or possessions

raiders—warriors who were skilled in finding supplies

reservations—lands set aside by the U.S. government for the forced removal of Native American communities from their original lands

settlers—people who move to live in a new region

territory—an area of land under the control of a government

traditions—customs, ideas, and beliefs handed down from one generation to the next

TO LEARN MORE

AT THE LIBRARY

Barnes, N.C. *The Apache*. Minneapolis, Minn.: Pop!, 2025.

Marcks, Betty. *The Navajo*. Minneapolis, Minn.: Bellwether Media, 2024.

Sonneborn, Liz. *The Hopi*. Minneapolis, Minn.: Bellwether Media, 2024.

ON THE WEB

Factsurfer.com gives you a safe, fun way to find more information.

1. Go to www.factsurfer.com.

2. Enter "the Apache" into the search box and click 🔍.

3. Select your book cover to see a list of related content.

INDEX